REBECCA
LOBO

REBECCA
LOBO

A. Rose McHugh
THE CHILD'S WORLD®, INC.

ON THE COVER...

Front cover: Rebecca thinks about the current game against the Los Angeles Sparks during a time out.
Page 2: Rebecca points to one of her New York Liberty teammates before passing the ball.

Library of Congress Cataloging-in-Publication Data
McHugh, A. Rose.
Rebecca Lobo / by A. Rose McHugh.
p. cm.
Includes index.
ISBN 1-56766-831-3 (lib. reinforced : alk. paper)
1. Lobo, Rebecca—Juvenile literature.
2. Basketball players—United States—Biography—Juvenile literature.
3. Women basketball players—United States—Biography—Juvenile literature.
[1. Lobo, Rebecca. 2. Basketball players. 3. Women—Biography.]   I. Title.
GV884.L6 M35 2000
796.323'092—dc21
00-038430

PHOTO CREDITS

© AP/Wide World Photos: 6, 9, 10, 13, 15, 16, 20, 22
© Michael Zito/SportsChrome-USA: cover, 2, 19

TABLE OF CONTENTS

GROWING UP TALL

Boom, boom, boom! The sound of bouncing basketballs could be heard across the gym. It was practice time for the Southwick (Massachusetts) High School girls' basketball team. The team's tallest player shoots at the basket. Her name is Rebecca Lobo. She is a normal teenager. She is a member of the school band and plays the saxophone. She is good in school.

She has a brother named Jason. She has friends and likes to eat lasagna and ice cream. Oh, yes, and she likes to play basketball. Rebecca practices very hard. She is good, and she wants to get even better. When she was young, she was so tall and good in basketball that she would often play with boys. Many say she is the best player in all of Massachusetts. But just how good is she?

THE BEST PLAYER IN HIGH SCHOOL

When Rebecca played, she gave it her all. She played hard on both offense and defense. She was good at passing, **rebounding,** and blocking shots. And she was good at scoring. As a matter fact, she became the highest scoring player in Massachusetts' history. She even scored more points than any boy ever did!

Rebecca defends Sacramento Monarch Pamela McGee during a 1997 New York Liberty game.

Rebecca was so good, she was offered a basketball **scholarship** to attend college. Many colleges wanted Rebecca to play on their basketball team. A scholarship would help her pay for college. She picked the University of Connecticut. She would play on their basketball team called the Huskies. But could she be as good of a player in college as she was in high school? That's what she set out to prove.

PLAYING FOR THE HUSKIES

With Rebecca on the team, the Huskies were really good. They won most of their games. Their goal was to make it to the national **tournament.** This tournament is where the best college teams play. The winner of this tournament is the national champion. Rebecca wanted the Huskies to be national champions.

In 1992 and 1993, Rebecca and the Huskies made it to the national tournament but didn't win. In 1994, they won their first three tournament games, but then they lost to the University of North Carolina. Although the season was over, she showed that she was one of the top players in the nation. She led her team in scoring, rebounds, and blocked shots. She only had one year left to play for the Huskies. Would she reach her goal and win the national championship?

Rebecca pulls in a rebound during a 1995 game against Tennessee.

→

In 1995, she was her team's leader. She again led the team in scoring, rebounds, and blocked shots. She played so well that the Huskies didn't lose a single game. Their record was 35–0.

In the NCAA Tournament, the Huskies won their first 5 games. They had made it to the championship game against the University of Tennessee. The University of Tennessee's basketball team was called the Lady Volunteers. They were really good. Could the Huskies beat the Lady Volunteers?

It was a hard-fought game, but Lobo and the Huskies won 70–64. They won the national championship! When the tournament ended, Rebecca was selected as the tournament's Most Valuable Player. That was her last college basketball game.

Rebecca had left her mark on the Huskies. She was their all-time leader in rebounds and blocked shots. But most importantly, she helped the Huskies win the national championship. After the season, she was named National Player of the Year. But was she done playing basketball now that she was finished with college?

Rebecca celebrates after the Huskies won the 1995 NCAA Women's Final Four.

AN OLYMPIC DREAM

After college, Rebecca was picked to play on the women's Olympic basketball team. She was the youngest member. She was honored to be chosen to play with the best basketball players in the United States. Her goal was to win the gold medal. The U.S. team didn't win the gold medal at the previous Olympics, so Lobo wanted to show that she could help the team win the gold medal this time.

To prepare for the Olympics, Rebecca's team practiced and prepared more than any other Olympic team. They traveled all around the world and played the best teams they could find. They played more than 50 games and won them all. Heading into the Olympics, the team hadn't lost a game. But would Lobo and her team be as good in the Olympics? That's what the world was waiting to see.

Rebecca looks for a teammate to pass to during an exhibition game on November 5, 1995.

→

PLAYING FOR THE GOLD

In the Olympics, the U.S. team won their first seven games. They made it to the final game. The winner of this game would win the gold medal. Lobo still hadn't lost a game in more than two years. She said, "I've been fortunate to be on two incredible teams. I've just been blessed."

Most other players on the team were between 24 and 30 years old. When Rebecca was picked, she was just out of college and only 21. Because she was the youngest player on the team, she didn't play very much. Some people thought she deserved to play more but Lobo said, "This is about what this team can do for our country. It's not about what individuals can do for themselves. I think everybody is trying to win the gold medal."

There were 33,000 fans watching the championship game. The U.S. would have to play Brazil. Brazil had a very good team and would be tough to beat. It was a tough game, but the U.S. beat Brazil, 111–87. They had won the gold medal! When they won, the crowd cheered and yelled "U-S-A, U-S-A, U-S-A!" Lobo scored two points, making the only shot she took. After the game she said, "This is a crowning moment for this team and for women's basketball in the United States, because we brought the gold back home." Rebecca was now an Olympic champion!

Rebecca and teammate Lisa Leslie celebrate USA's win over Cuba in a game during the 1996 Olympics.

→

ON TO PROFESSIONAL BASKETBALL

After the Olympics, Rebecca was picked to play **professional** basketball. A professional basketball player is paid for playing. She agreed to play in the Women's National Basketball Association (WNBA). She was one of the first players in this league.

In 1997, the WNBA had its first season. Rebecca played for the New York Liberty. This was a brand-new team for Rebecca. She hadn't lost a basketball game in two years. Could she keep her **winning streak** going?

PLAYING FOR THE NEW YORK LIBERTY

With Rebecca on the team, the Liberty was a really good team. She was the center on her team. She kept her winning streak going. The Liberty won its first seven games. When people asked her about her long winning streak, she said, "I don't think about it all that much. I've been blessed."

Rebecca said, "It feels pretty good to be on a team where winning is the important thing, not who scores the most points or gets the headlines. That's what this team is about, and that's why this team is winning." Would her winning streak continue?

Rebecca goes after the ball under the Los Angeles Sparks' basket in a 1997 game.

Their next game was against the Phoenix Mercury. The Mercury had very good players. It was a tough game, and Rebecca missed most of her shots. She scored eight points, but this was not enough as the Liberty lost, 69–50. After the game she said, "It just feels awful to lose, streak or no streak. All I want to do is start another streak." Before that night, she had won an incredible 102 games in a row without a loss. This is the longest winning streak of any basketball player!

AN ALL-STAR PLAYER

In 1997, she was one of the top scorers for the Liberty. She led the team in rebounds and blocked shots. In 1998, she again led the Liberty in rebounds and blocked shots. Going into the 1999 season she was hoping to be picked to play in the first WNBA **All-Star** Game.

But in the Liberty's first game of the year, she got hurt. It was on June 10, 1999 against the Cleveland Rockers. She twisted her knee and had to leave the game. Her knee was hurt so badly, that she wasn't able to play another game all year. Her coach said, "Rebecca is an [important] part of both our team's offense and defense. Losing her for the rest of the season is difficult. She was having a great training camp and was playing very well."

Rebecca goes up for a shot during a New York Liberty game.

And what about the All-Star Game? Even though she was injured, she was voted as a starter for the 1999 All-Star Game. And although she didn't play, she cheered for her teammates. She waited all year for her knee to heal. But prior to the 2000 season, she injured her knee again. A member of the Liberty said, "I'm confident that Rebecca will work even harder to come back from this stronger and even more competitive than ever."

Rebecca is determined to come back and help the Liberty in another great season. She just can't wait to start playing again!

Rebecca talks with reporters during a practice before the 1999 All-Star Game.